WALLPAPER PATTERNS

GINGKO PRESS

First Published by Gingko Press in the United States of America in 2009
by arrangement with Liaoning Science and Technology Publishing House

First   Edition
Gingko Press, Inc.
1321 Fifth Street
Berkeley, CA 94710, USA

Phone (510) 898 1195
Fax (510) 898 1195
www.gingkopress.com

ISBN: 978-1-58423-340-4

Editor：Chai Xiuming
Designer：Zhao Cong

Printed in China

Contents

Foreword

As a specific art form that possesses both artistic and practical features, patterned and illustrated wallcoverings have become an integral part of people's lives. Since the Mid-18th century, patterned materials and wallpapers have been mass-produced, and over time, the forms have undergone constant change in step with economic and culture trends. However, patterns will always be a primary element no matter how the materials and production processes change. In the modern era, an age in which saturated graphics prevail, paper is no longer the only medium for the patterns which are much evolved from their traditional styles. Decorations emulating the effect of wallpaper are very popular, with patterns ranging from simple lines or colorful blocks to frenetic, natural or random arrangements. Such patterns immediately enhance a quiet living space or bring energy to a common area or meeting room. Wallpaper Patterns principally portrays patterns designed for wallpapers or as technical paintings applied directly on walls. The projects are carefully selected, and each one is presented as a vector graphic file on the accompanying CD-Rom. A valuable reference book for designers and everyone who likes patterns.

TITLE: The Wonderfactory
DESIGNER: 212box Architecture PC
COUNTRY: USA

TITLE: The Wonderfactory
DESIGNER: 212box Architecture PC
COUNTRY: USA

009

TITLE: Skin
DESIGNER: Katrin Olina
COUNTRY: Italy

TITLE: Home Show
DESIGNER: Greg Natale
COUNTRY: Australia
WALLPAPER PRINT: Southbeach
MANUFACTURER: Signature Prints

012

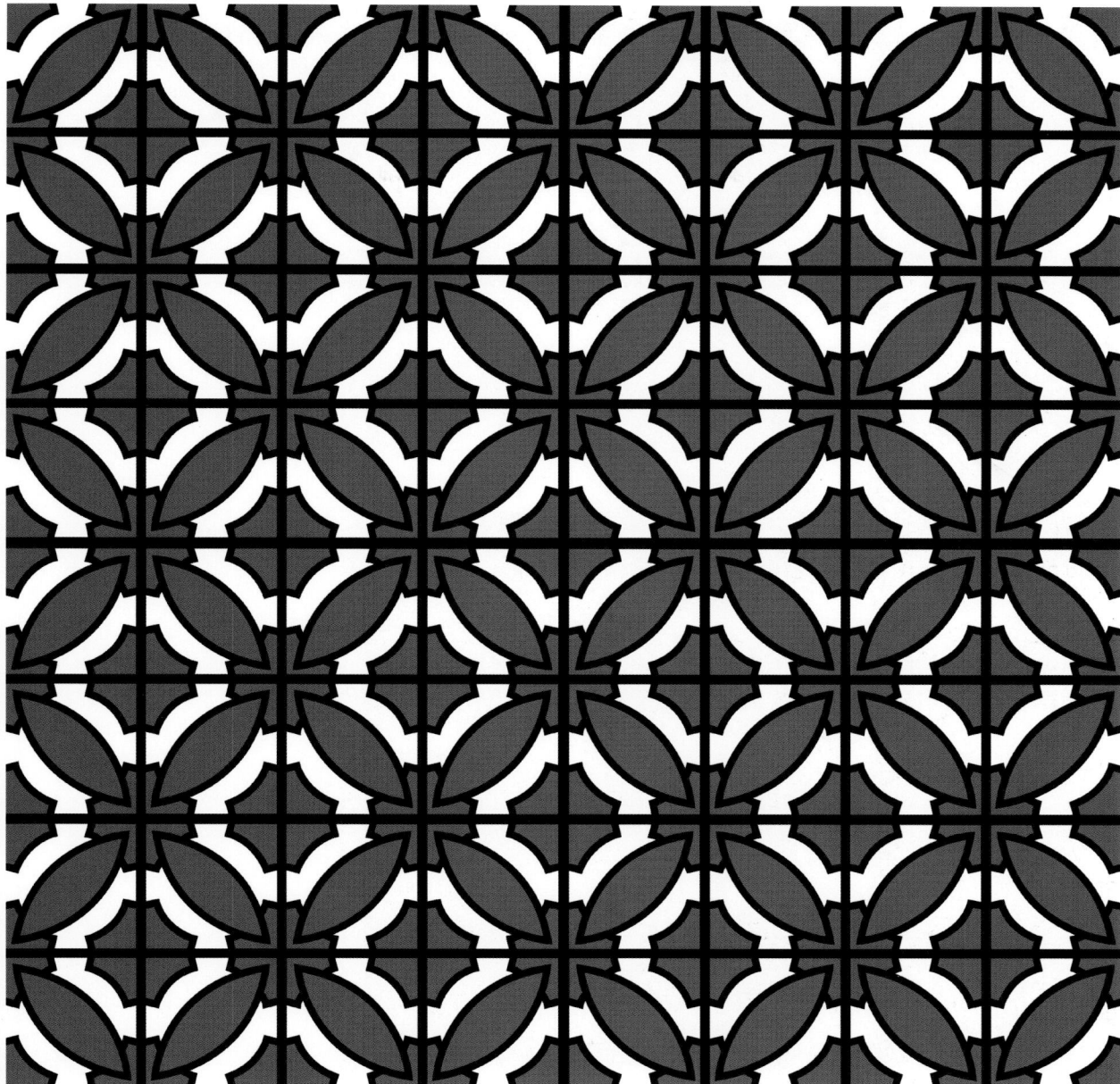

013

014

TITLE: Mister Goodbar
DESIGNER: Greg Natale
WALLPAPER DESIGNER: Florence Broadhurst
COUNTRY: Australia
WALLPAPER PRINT: Geometric G
PRINTED BY: Signature Prints

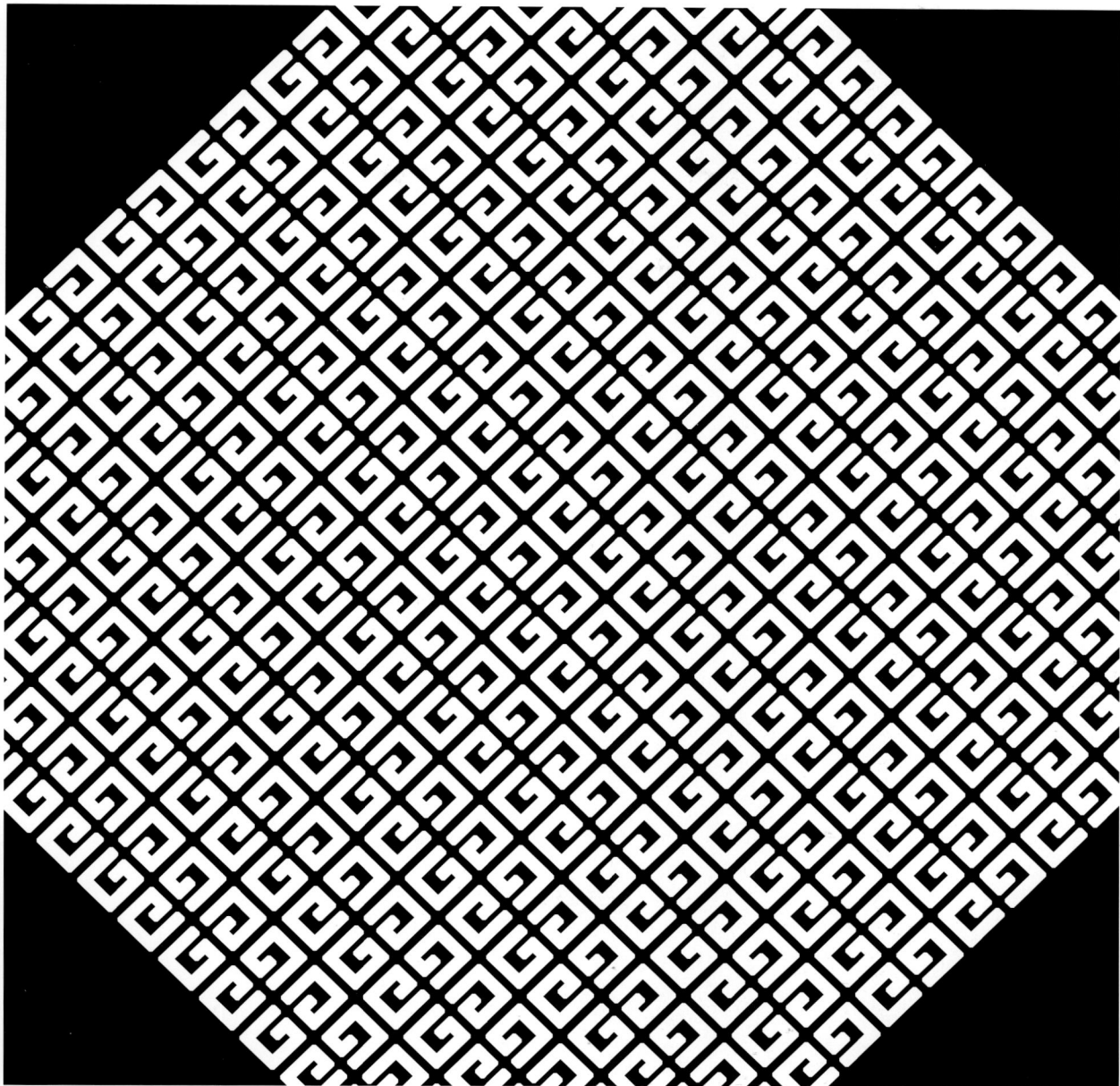

TITLE: Mister Goodbar
DESIGNER: Greg Natale
COUNTRY: Australia
WALLPAPER PRINT: Woodstock
MANUFACTURER: Cole & Son

018

TITLE: Splash
DESIGNER: Greg Natale
COUNTRY: Australia
WALLPAPER PRINT: Vintage
MANUFACTURER: Unknown
SUPPLIER: Twentieth Century Modern By Ken Kneale

020

TITLE: Hunter Bar
DESIGNER: Greg Natale
COUNTRY: Australia
WALLPAPER PRINT: Palmyra
MANUFACTURER: Osborne & Little

TITLE: Superwoman

DESIGNER: Greg Natale

WALLPAPER DESIGNER: Tord Boontje

COUNTRY: Australia

STICKER PRINT: Tord Boontje Window Sticker

MANUFACTURER: Moroso

023

TITLE: Superwoman
DESIGNER: Greg Natale
WALLPAPER DESIGNER: Tord Boontje
COUNTRY: Australia
FABRIC PRINT: Prince
MANUFACTURER: Kvadrat

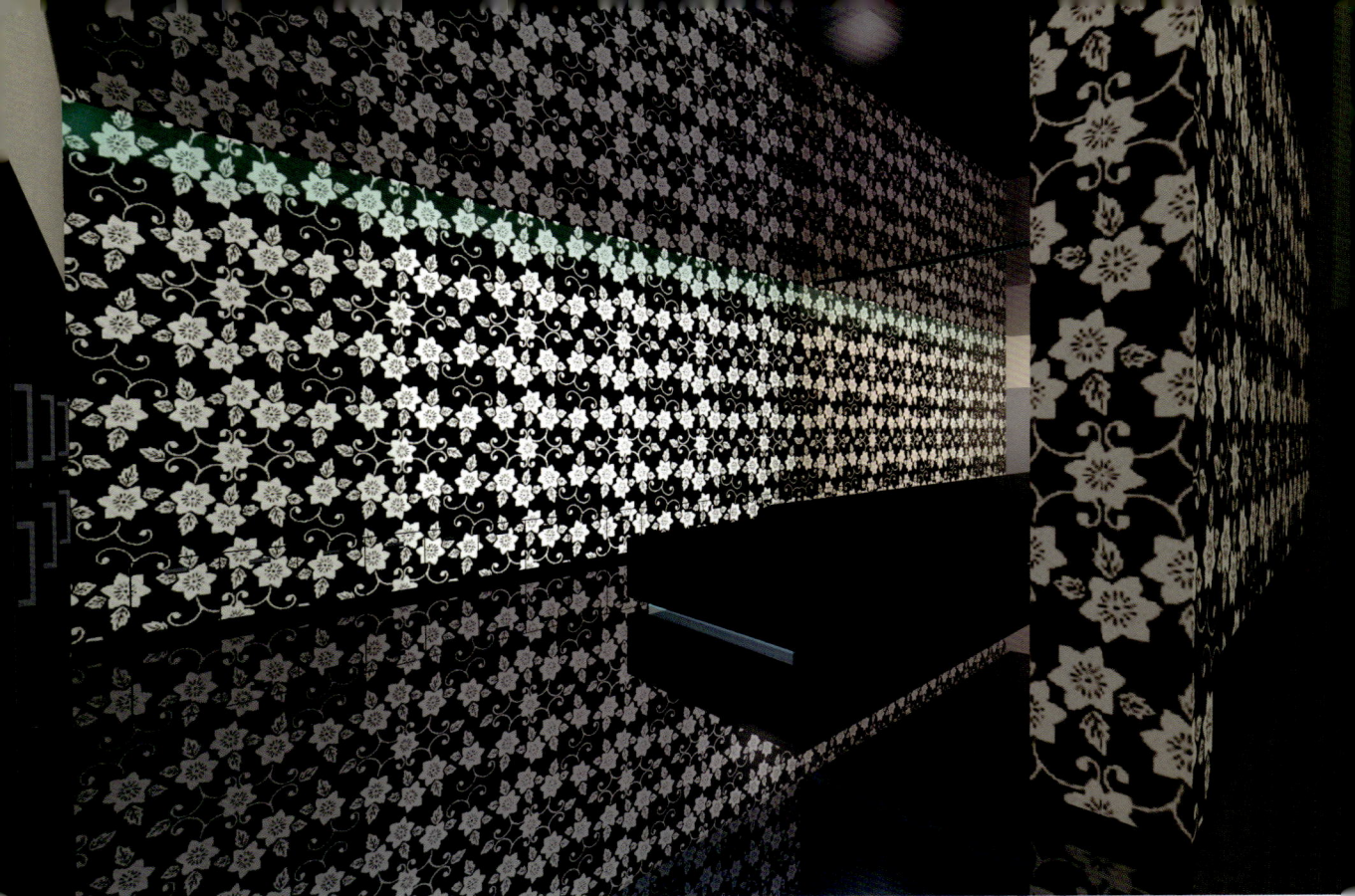

TITLE: Apartment S

DESIGNER: Ippolito Fleitz Group

COUNTRY: Germany

TITLE: Bird Branch

DESIGNERS: Timorous Beasties: Alistair McAuley And Paul Simmons

COUNTRY: UK

DESCRIPTION: Sold as set of 6 panels. Panel dimensions: 6 panels of 520mm by 3300mm.

TITLE: Branch Out
DESIGNER: Timorous Beasties: Alistair Mcauley And Paul Simmons
COUNTRY: UK

TITLE: Black Flower
DESIGNER: Timorous Mcauley And Paul Simmons
COUNTRY: UK

032

TITLE: Bloody Hell Wallpaper Mint
DESIGNER: Timorous Beasties: Alistair McAuley And Paul Simmons
COUNTRY: UK

033

TITLE: Butterfly

DESIGNER: Timorous Beasties: Alistair Mcauley And Paul Simmons

COUNTRY: UK

DESCRIPTION: The wallpaper is printed using different ink to overlap one another to create an almost embossed effect.

TITLE: Damask
DESIGNER: Timorous Beasties: Alistair Mcauley And Paul Simmons
COUNTRY: UK

TITLE: Decouper 1

DESIGNER: Timorous Beasties: Alistair McAuley And Paul Simmons

COUNTRY: UK

DESCRIPTION:

The new "Découper Toile" collection from Timorous Beasties takes on the chinioserie style which originates from the18th century.

This new collection features old men, youths, workers, shoppers, pregnant mothers, cyclists, and tramps, all of whom are richly silhouetted onto a decorative backdrop of traditional pattern. Découper means 'to cut out' in French, which is also the source for the term 'découpage'.

Découpage was very popular in the18th century in Britain with the upper and burgeoning middle classes. Images were cut from valuable prints and lacquered onto hatboxes, gift boxes and even walls. Unlike the original sentimental patterns that were popular in the 1700s, Timorous Beasties have used generic everyday urban images of contemporary life to make an engaging and original collection of printed fabrics and wallpapers that challenges both old and new ideas of class, wealth and taste.

TITLE Decouper 2
DESIGNER Timorous Beasties: Alistair Mcauley And Paul Simmons
COUNTRY UK

TITLE: Decouper 3
DESIGNER: Timorous Beasties: Alistair Mcauley And Paul Simmons
COUNTRY: UK

TITLE: Euro Damask

DESIGNER: Timorous Beasties:
Alistair McAuley And Paul Simmons

COUNTRY: UK

DESCRIPTION:

The wallpaper is designed by using the silhouettes of different European countries and their coastlines, merged into the shape of a traditional Damask echoing images employed by the psychoanalyst, Rorschach.

TITLE: Fresco

DESIGNER: Timorous Beasties: Alistair Mcauley And Paul Simmons

COUNTRY: UK

TITLE: Insect
DESIGNER: Timorous Beasties: Alistair Mcauley And Paul Simmons
COUNTRY: UK

TITLE: London Toile

DESIGNER: Timorous Beasties: Alistair McAuley And Paul Simmons

COUNTRY: UK

DESCRIPTION:

The London Toile is the second Toile that Timorous Beasties have produced, the first being "Glasgow Toile". It is aesthetically different and its reference is from the images of "islands" that are often found in the original Toiles.

The London Toile was designed from a love of London and a love of the old Toiles that were produced in pre-revolutionary and post industrial France, in the small town of Jouey in the 1770s. Like the original Toile, the London Toile was designed using the same techniques by separating the drawings, producing extra depth and texture and leaving gaps in the artwork to create more tones when the inks overlap one another.

Some imageries in the original Toiles were sinister; they depicted scenes that were then "contemporary", but we now consider those traditional. Some scenes showed the factory at Jouey, and other rural scenes showed workers' relaxing, drinking, dancing, and womanising. Timorous Beasties have not actually changed much in the Toile concept, but have updated the references from the contemporary urban.

TITLE: Mc Gegan Rose

DESIGNER: Timorous Beasties: Alistair Mcauley And Paul Simmons

COUNTRY: UK

051

TITLE: Napoleon Bee
DESIGNER: Timorous Beasties: Alistair Mcauley And Paul Simmons
COUNTRY: UK

054

TITLE: Pheasant
DESIGNER: Timorous Beasties: Alistair Mcauley And Paul Simmons
COUNTRY: UK

TITLE: Leaf

DESIGNER: Timorous Beasties: Alistair McAuley And Paul Simmons

COUNTRY: UK

DESCRIPTION:

The superwide wallpapers are hand-printed onto a non-woven paper which has recently been made available on the market. As non-woven paper could not be buckled, it enables us to produce wallpapers that have the same width as fabrics.

The designs we have produced are all in large scale, and have all the Timorous Beasties hallmarks. Some of them could be seen as a wayward take on the often "twee" world of textiles, with heavily illustrative insects, triffid-like plants and lizards swirl in intricate patterns and repeats that are simply printed in a tonal range of Black, Grey, Silver and White on cream.

057

TITLE: Bird Cage
DESIGNER: Timorous Mcauley And Paul Simmons
COUNTRY: UK

TITLE: Thistle
DESIGNER: Timorous Beasties: Alistair Mcauley And Paul Simmons
COUNTRY: UK

TITLE: Orchid Wallpaper Black

DESIGNER: Timorous Beasties: Alistair McAuley And Paul Simmons

COUNTRY: UK

DESCRIPTION:

Extravagant 4 screen hand-printed wallpaper.

With the Oriental Orchid design, the organic meets the graphic: delicate orchids boldly intertwine with subtle print images from a Japanese Manga cartoon, depicting activities of depraved sexual appetite. The most sexually graphic points of focus in the Manga are draped with flowers, which allude to a commonly perceived sexual association with orchids.

Building overlays of matt and gloss inks in this subtle confluence of the organic & graphic, the Oriental Orchid design illustrates the unique qualities only achieved through hand printing.

063

064

TITLE: Orchid Wallpaper Black
DESIGNER: Timorous Beasties: Alistair Mcauley And Paul Simmons
COUNTRY: UK

TITLE: Good Spirits Room 107
DESIGNER: Rinzen – Australia
CLIENT: Hotel Fox
COUNTRY: Denmark

068

TITLE: Dryads-Room 307

DESIGNER: Rinzen – Australia

CLIENT: Hotel Fox

COUNTRY: Denmark

TITLE: Supanova-Room 314
DESIGNER: Pandarosa – Australia
CLIENT: Hotel Fox
COUNTRY: Denmark

070

TITLE: Staircase
DESIGNER: Birgit Amadori – Germany
CLIENT: Hotel Fox
COUNTRY: Denmark

TITLE: Mori-Room 112
DESIGNER: Kinpro – Japan
CLIENT: Hotel Fox
COUNTRY: Denmark

072

TITLE: Ecstasy-Room 206
DESIGNER: WK interact – France
CLIENT: Hotel Fox
COUNTRY: Denmark

073

TITLE: Sensuality-Room 311
DESIGNER: WK interact – France
CLIENT: Hotel Fox
COUNTRY: Denmark

TITLE: Imataca-Room 115
DESIGNER: MASA – Venezuela
CLIENT: Hotel Fox
COUNTRY: Denmark

TITLE: Tinkp Eepe-Room 116
DESIGNER: Freaklüb – Spain
CLIENT: Hotel Fox
COUNTRY: Denmark

076

TITLE: King's Forest-Room 217
DESIGNER: Birgit Amadori - Germany
CLIENT: Hotel Fox
COUNTRY: Denmark

TITLE: Big Birds With Big Eyes-Room 205
DESIGNER: Hort – Germany
CLIENT: Hotel Fox
COUNTRY: Denmark

TITLE: You Are A Baby-Room 202
DESIGNER: Boris Hoppek – Germany
CLIENT: Hotel Fox
COUNTRY: Denmark

079

TITLE: The Traveller-Room 211
DESIGNER: Rinzen – Australia
CLIENT: Hotel Fox
COUNTRY: Denmark

TITLE: Japanese Garden-Room 212
DESIGNER: Tokidoki – Italy
CLIENT: Hotel Fox
COUNTRY: Denmark

82% of all European hotel rooms feature a romantic landscape painting

77% of all hotel rooms in Denmark have white walls.

Last year, 5 out of 10 people said that this bed was firm enough. 3 out of 10 said that the bed was too soft. The rest had absolutely no opinion.

TITLE: Complexity-Reliability-Room 414
DESIGNER: E-Types – Denmark
CLIENT: Hotel Fox
COUNTRY: Denmark

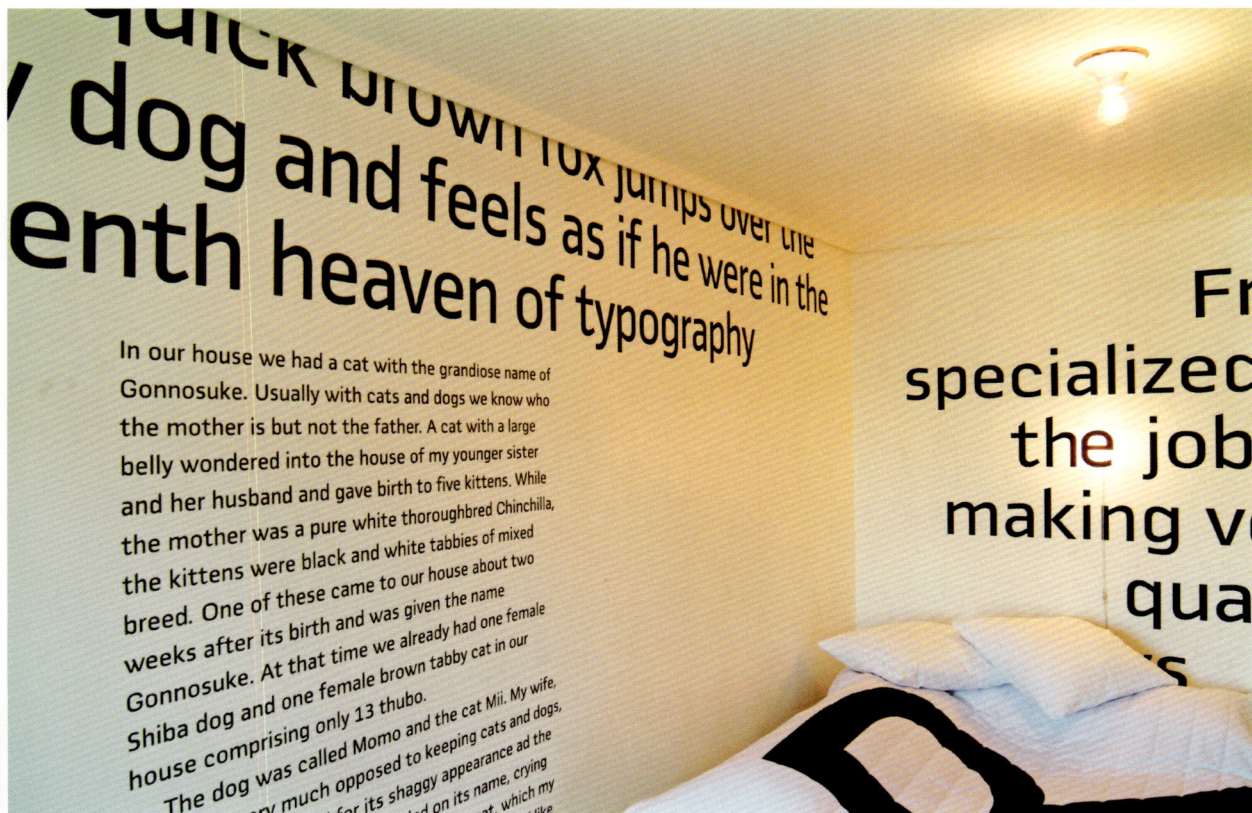

quick brown fox jumps over the lazy dog and feels as if he were in the seventh heaven of typography

In our house we had a cat with the grandiose name of Gonnosuke. Usually with cats and dogs we know who the mother is but not the father. A cat with a large belly wondered into the house of my younger sister and her husband and gave birth to five kittens. While the mother was a pure white thoroughbred Chinchilla, the kittens were black and white tabbies of mixed breed. One of these came to our house about two weeks after its birth and was given the name Gonnosuke. At that time we already had one female Shiba dog and one female brown tabby cat in our house comprising only 13 thubo.
The dog was called Momo and the cat Mii. My wife, very much opposed to keeping cats and dogs, ... for its shaggy appearance ad the ... ed on its name, crying ... cat, which my ...

Fr specialized the job making v qua

083

TITLE: Self-confidence-Room 304
DESIGNER: E-Types – Denmark
CLIENT: Hotel Fox
COUNTRY: Denmark

TITLE: Two Swans-Room 214
DESIGNER: Friendswithyou – USA
CLIENT: Hotel Fox
COUNTRY: Denmark

085

TITLE: Heidi-Room 409
DESIGNER: Benjamin Güdel – Switzerland
CLIENT: Hotel Fox
COUNTRY: Denmark

TITLE: Clubs-The Secret Palace-Room 309

DESIGNER: Container – UK

CLIENT: Hotel Fox

COUNTRY: Denmark

089

TITLE: Woo Flart-Room 403
DESIGNER: Freaklüb – Spain
CLIENT: Hotel Fox
COUNTRY: Denmark

TITLE: East Side Grero Sound System-Room 308
DESIGNER: MASA – Venezuela
CLIENT: Hotel Fox
COUNTRY: Denmark

TITLE: Sleep Well-Room 106
DESIGNER: Geneviève Gauckler – France
CLIENT: Hotel Fox
COUNTRY: Denmark

TITLE: Wa-Room 404
DESIGNER: Kinpro – Japan
CLIENT: Hotel Fox
COUNTRY: Denmark

TITLE: Lifelines-Room 405
DESIGNER: Pandarosa – Australia
CLIENT: Hotel Fox
COUNTRY: Denmark

094

TITLE: Harmony's Helm-Room 302
DESIGNER: Friendswithyou – USA
CLIENT: Hotel Fox
COUNTRY: Denmark

095

TITLE: Yume-Room 312
DESIGNER: Kinpro – Japan
CLIENT: Hotel Fox
COUNTRY: Denmark

TITLE: Boxing-Room 504
DESIGNER: Boris Hoppek – Germany
CLIENT: Hotel Fox
COUNTRY: Denmark

097

TITLE: Hearts-The Royal Wedding-Room 502

DESIGNER: Container – UK

CLIENT: Hotel Fox

COUNTRY: Denmark

TITLE: Chance-Room 209
DESIGNER: Antoine et Manuel - France
CLIENT: Hotel Fox
COUNTRY: Denmark

TITLE: Clubs-The Royal Garden-Room 103
DESIGNER: Container – UK
CLIENT: Hotel Fox
COUNTRY: Denmark

TITLE: King Albino Room-Room 102
DESIGNER: Friendswithyou – USA
CLIENT: Hotel Fox
COUNTRY: Denmark

TITLE: Spring Grove-Room 412
DESIGNER: Anke Vera Zink – Germany
CLIENT: Hotel Fox
COUNTRY: Denmark

102

TITLE: King's Court 1-Room 509
DESIGNER: Birgit Amadori – Germany
CLIENT: Hotel Fox
COUNTRY: Denmark

103

TITLE: King's Court 2-Room 510
DESIGNER: Birgit Amadori – Germany
CLIENT: Hotel Fox
COUNTRY: Denmark

104

TITLE: Back To School
DESIGNER: Andreas Samuelsson
COUNTRY: Sweden

TITLE: Untitled

DESIGNER: Andreas Samuelsson

COUNTRY: Sweden

TITLE: Choose Shoes
DESIGNER: Andreas Samuelsson
COUNTRY: Sweden

106

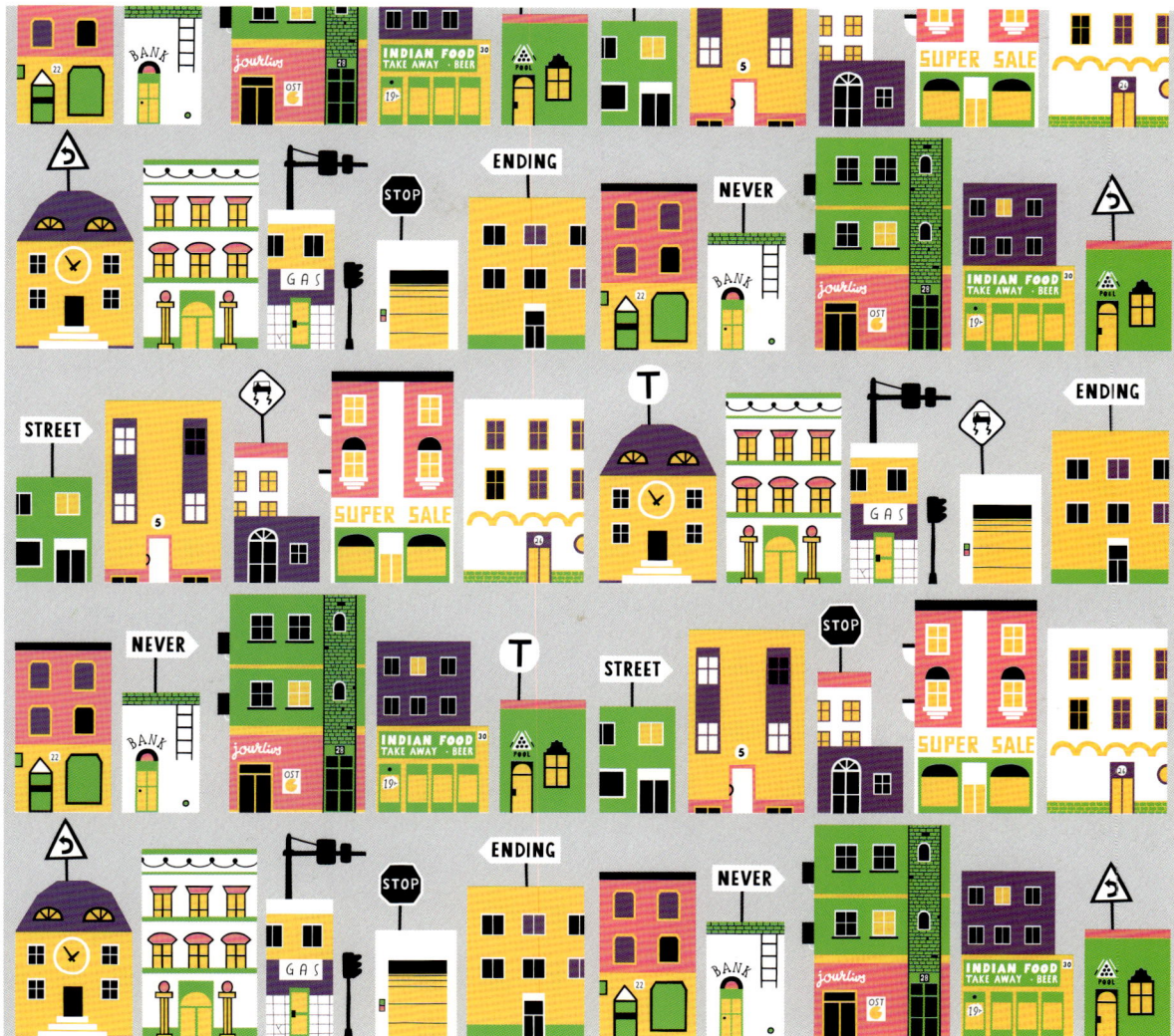

107

TITLE: Never Ending Street
DESIGNER: Andreas Samuelsson
COUNTRY: Sweden

TITLE: 4 You
DESIGNER: Andreas Samuelsson
COUNTRY: Sweden

TITLE: Leafage
DESIGNER: Xiuming Chai
COUNTRY: China

116

118

TITLE: Revival
DESIGNER: Xiuming Chai
COUNTRY: China

TITLE: Tree And Birds
DESIGNER: Xiuming Chai
COUNTRY: China

119

120

TITLE: Water Lily-1
DESIGNER: Xiuming Chai
COUNTRY: China

122

124

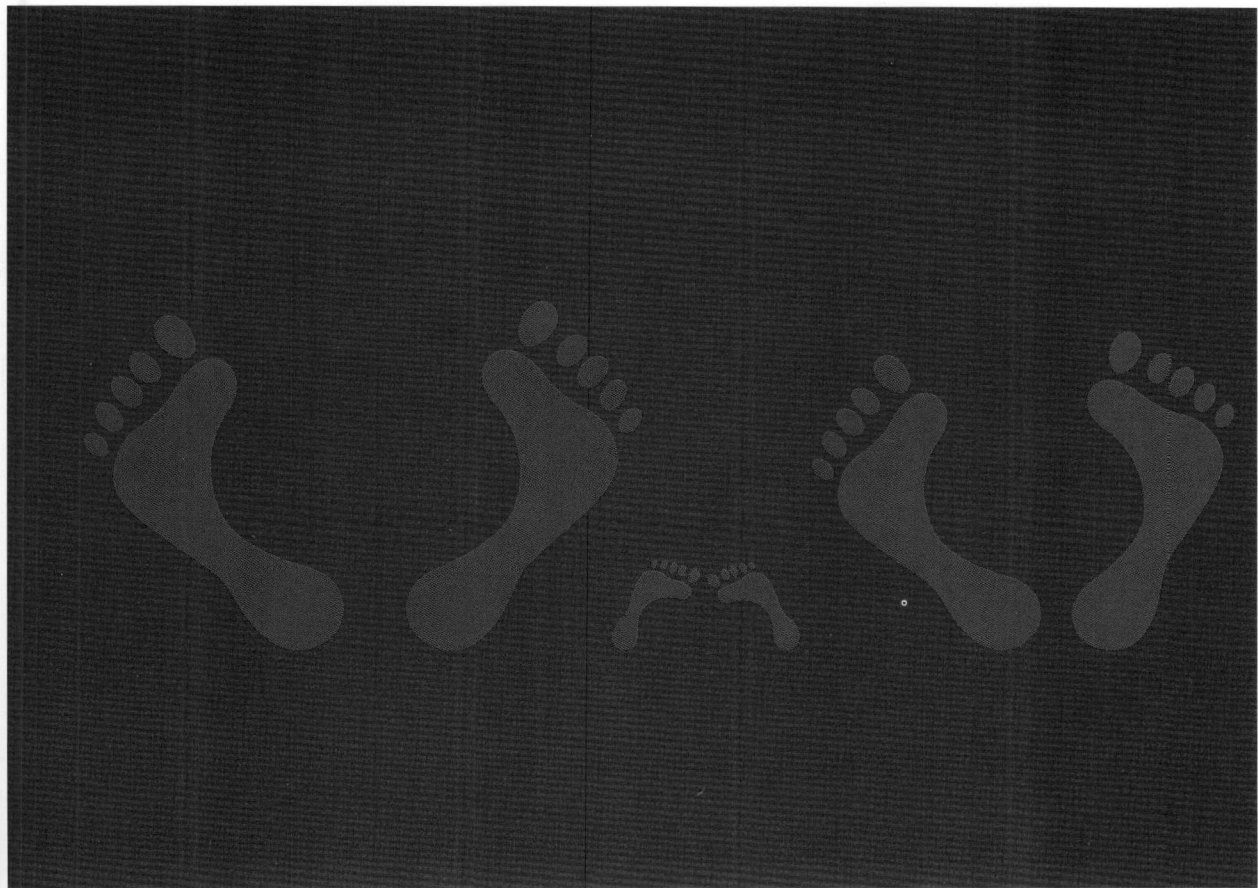

TITLE: Bamboo
DESIGNER: Xiuming Chai
COUNTRY: China

129

TITLE: Facile And Graceful
DESIGNER: Xiuming Chai
COUNTRY: China

130

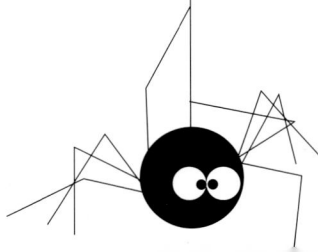

TITLE: Plum Blossom
DESIGNER: Xiuming Chai
COUNTRY: China

TITLE: Calla
DESIGNER: Xiuming Chai
COUNTRY: China

TITLE: Leaves
DESIGNER: Xiuming Chai
COUNTRY: China

140

TITLE: Branch For Cartier Jewelry Window Display
DESIGNER: Atelier Lzc
COUNTRY: France

142

TITLE: Stickers For French Children Wear Shop : DPAM 1
DESIGNER: Atelier Lzc
COUNTRY: France

TITLE: Stickers For French Children Wear Shop : DPAM 2
DESIGNER: Atelier Lzc
COUNTRY: France

TITLE: Stickers For French Children Wear Shop : DPAM 3
DESIGNER: Atelier Lzc
COUNTRY: France

145

TITLE Pattern For Sliding Doors Company : Cabinet
DESIGNER Atelier Lzc
COUNTRY France

146

TITLE: "pigeons" Stickers
DESIGNER: Atelier Lzc
COUNTRY: France

149

TITLE: Garden Sticker
DESIGNER: Atelier Lzc
COUNTRY: France

150

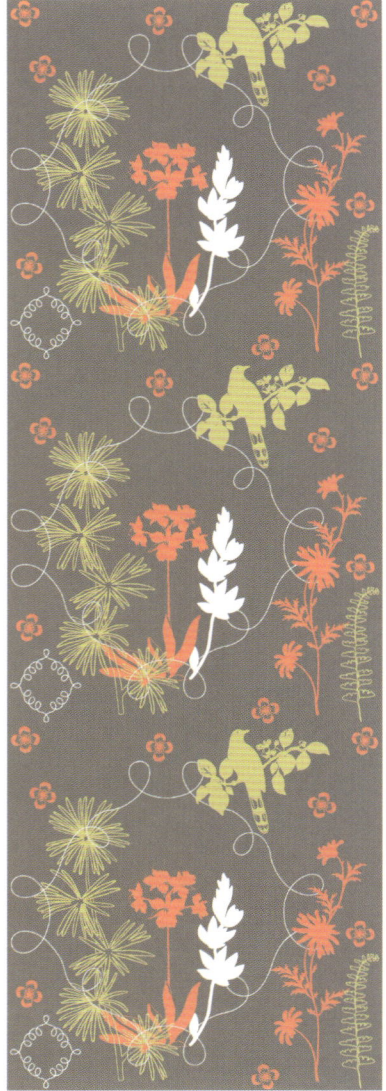

TITLE: Wallpaper

DESIGNER: Atelier Lzc

COUNTRY: France

TITLE: Pattern For Slate Mats
DESIGNER: Atelier Lzc
COUNTRY: France

TITLE: Crying Rain
DESIGNER: Marie Hansen
COUNTRY: Denmark
WEBSITE: www.ordinarymary.dk

TITLE: Tree Life Cycle
DESIGNER: MY.S
COUNTRY: Brazil
DESCRIPTION:

The idea was to represent the stages of a growing tree.

161

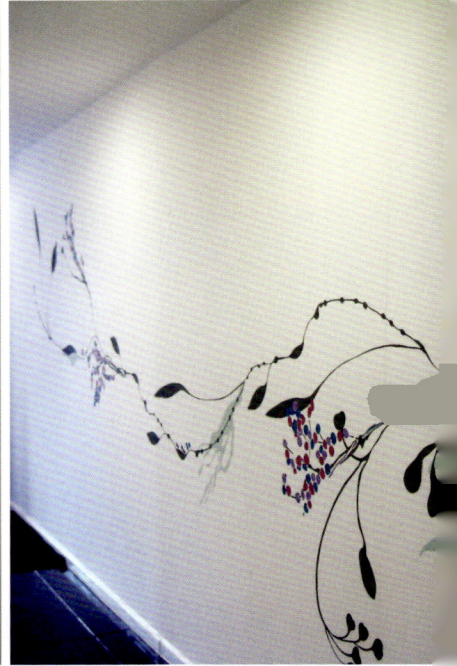

TITLE: Spring

DESIGNER: MY.S

COUNTRY: Brazil

CLIENT: Spezzato

DESCRIPTION:

This artwork was painted on a showroom's corridor of Spezzato (a brazilian fashion brand for ladies) for the Spring/Summer 2009 collection.

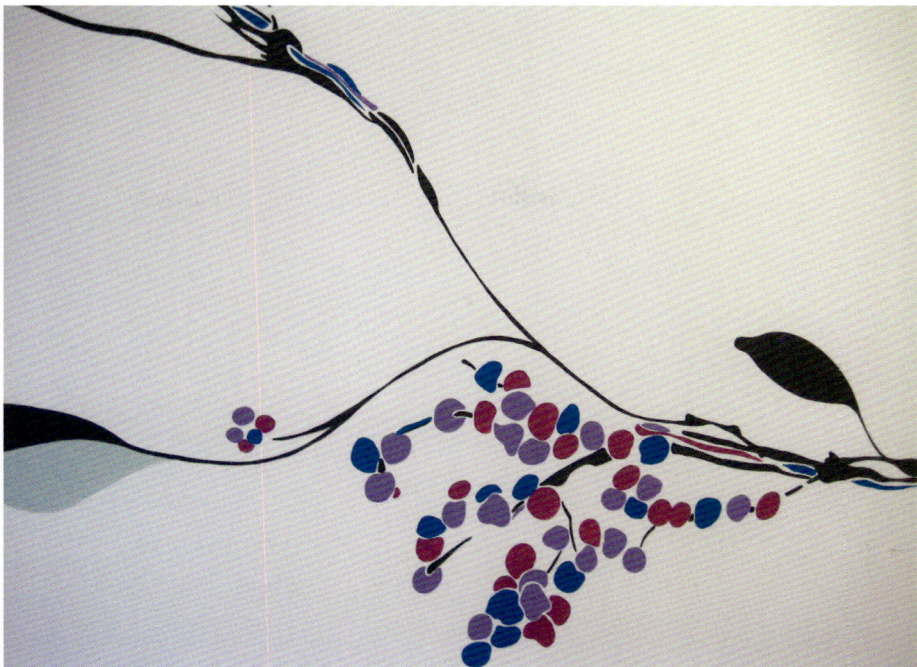

163

TITLE: Sky

DESIGNER: MY.S

COUNTRY: Brazil

DESCRIPTION:

A wall painting developed to transform a simple TV Room into a comfortable and cozy place.

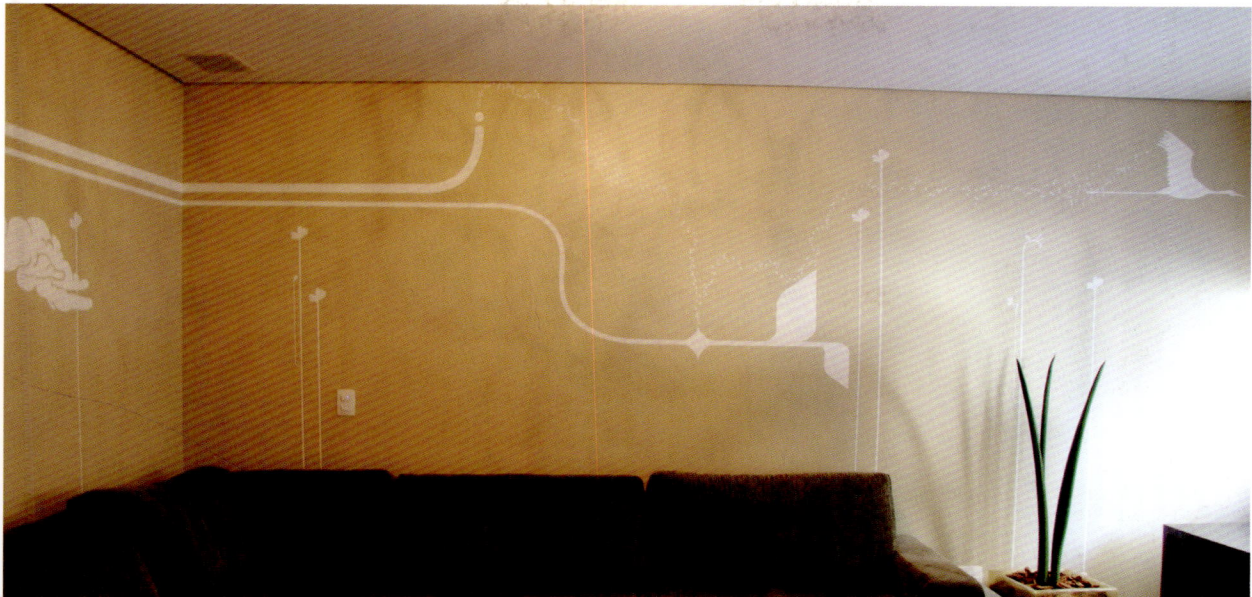

TITLE: Gotisso
DESIGNER: MY.S
COUNTRY: Brazil
CLIENT: Gotisso Oriental Food
DESCRIPTION:

A wall Painting creating a comfortable atmosphere for a Japanese restaurant based in São Paulo, Brazil.

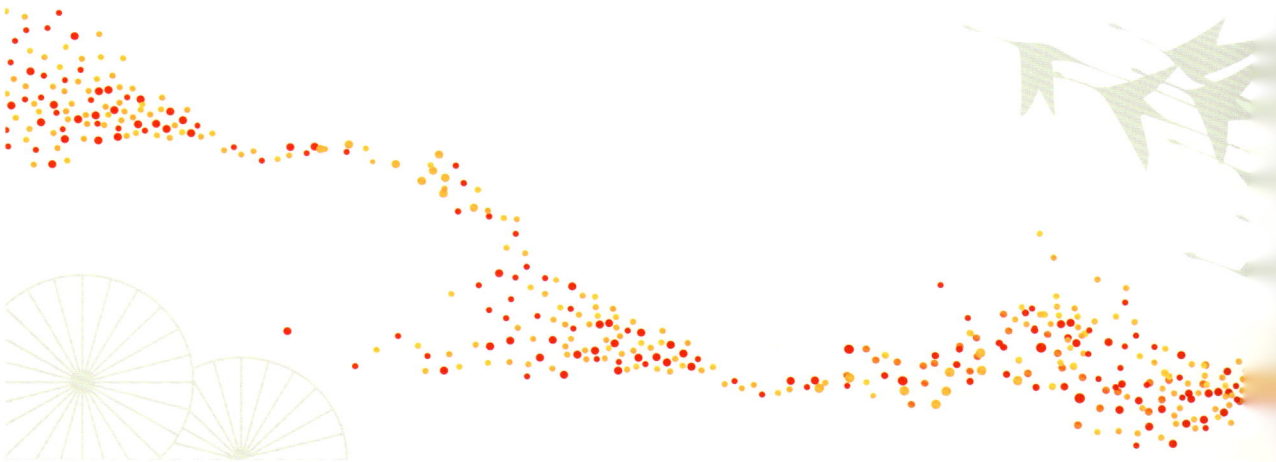

166

168

TITLE: Fabbrica
DESIGNER: Tjep.
COUNTRY: The Netherlands

TITLE: ROC Economy - A Temple For Economics
DESIGNER: Tjep.
COUNTRY: Netherlands

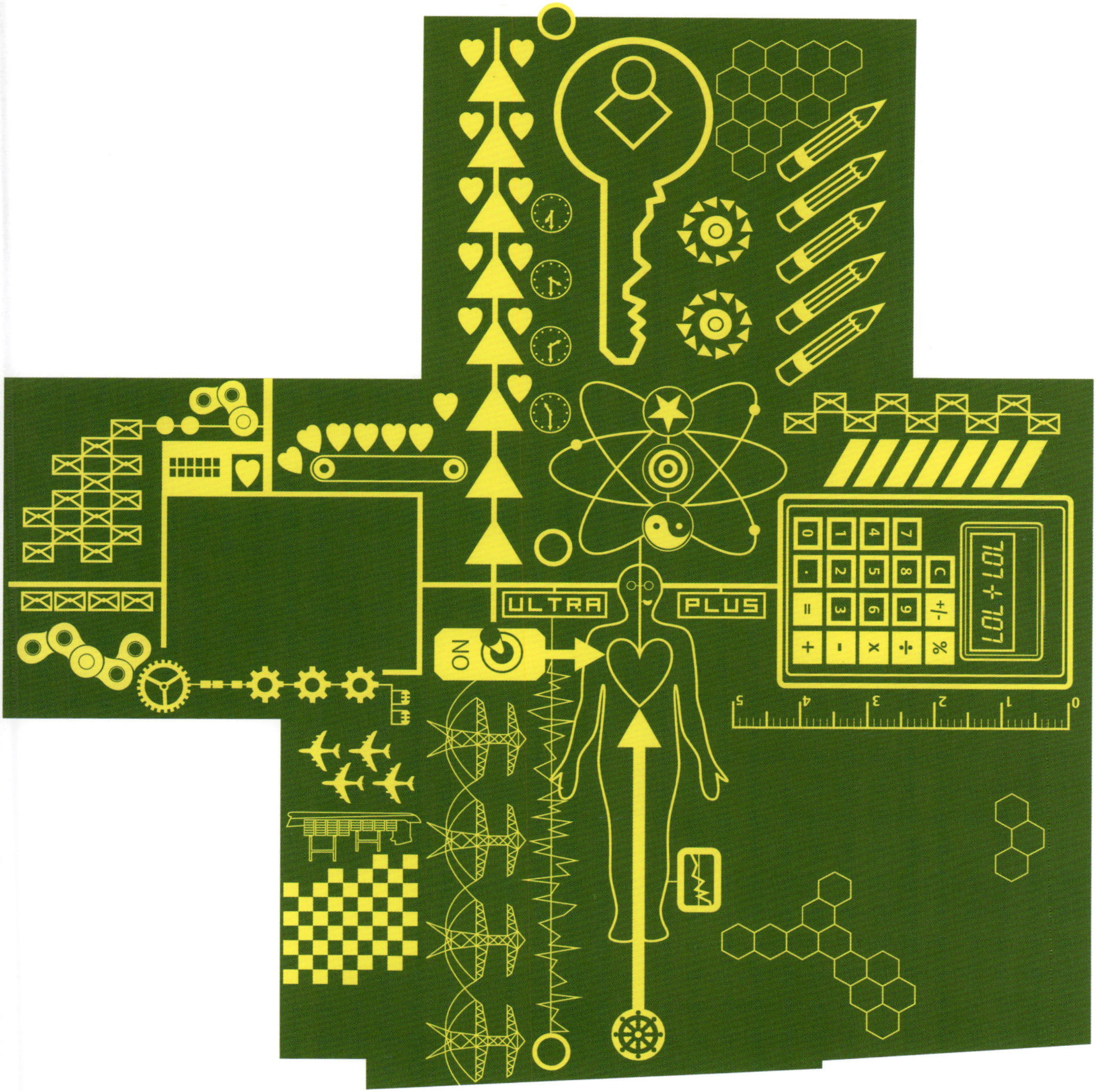
ULTRA
PLUS
ON

172

TITLE: Peacock Dinner Club
DESIGNER: Olssonlyckefors Architects
COUNTRY: Sweden

173

TITLE: Killah
DESIGNER: Studio 63 Architecture + Design
COUNTRY: Italy

175

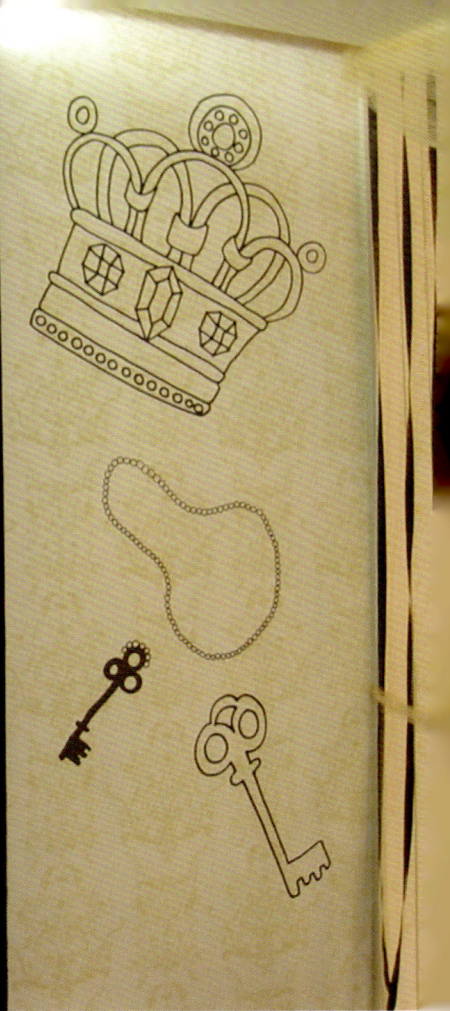

176

TITLE: Sixty
DESIGNER: Studio 63 Architecture + Design
COUNTRY: Italy

TITLE: KILLAH
DESIGNER: Studio 63 Architecture + Design
COUNTRY: Italy

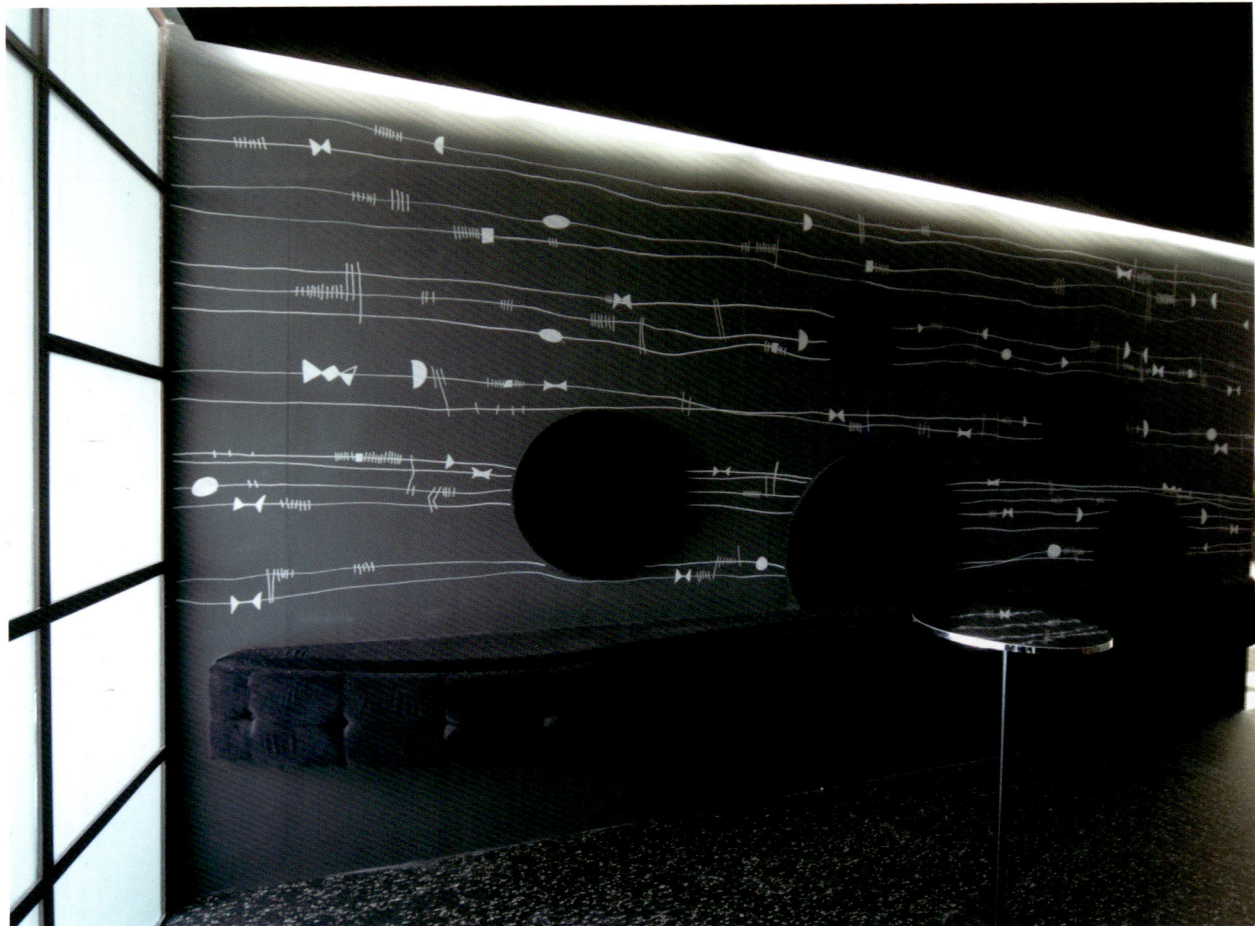

180

TITLE: Sixty
DESIGNER: Studio 63 Architecture + Design
COUNTRY: Italy

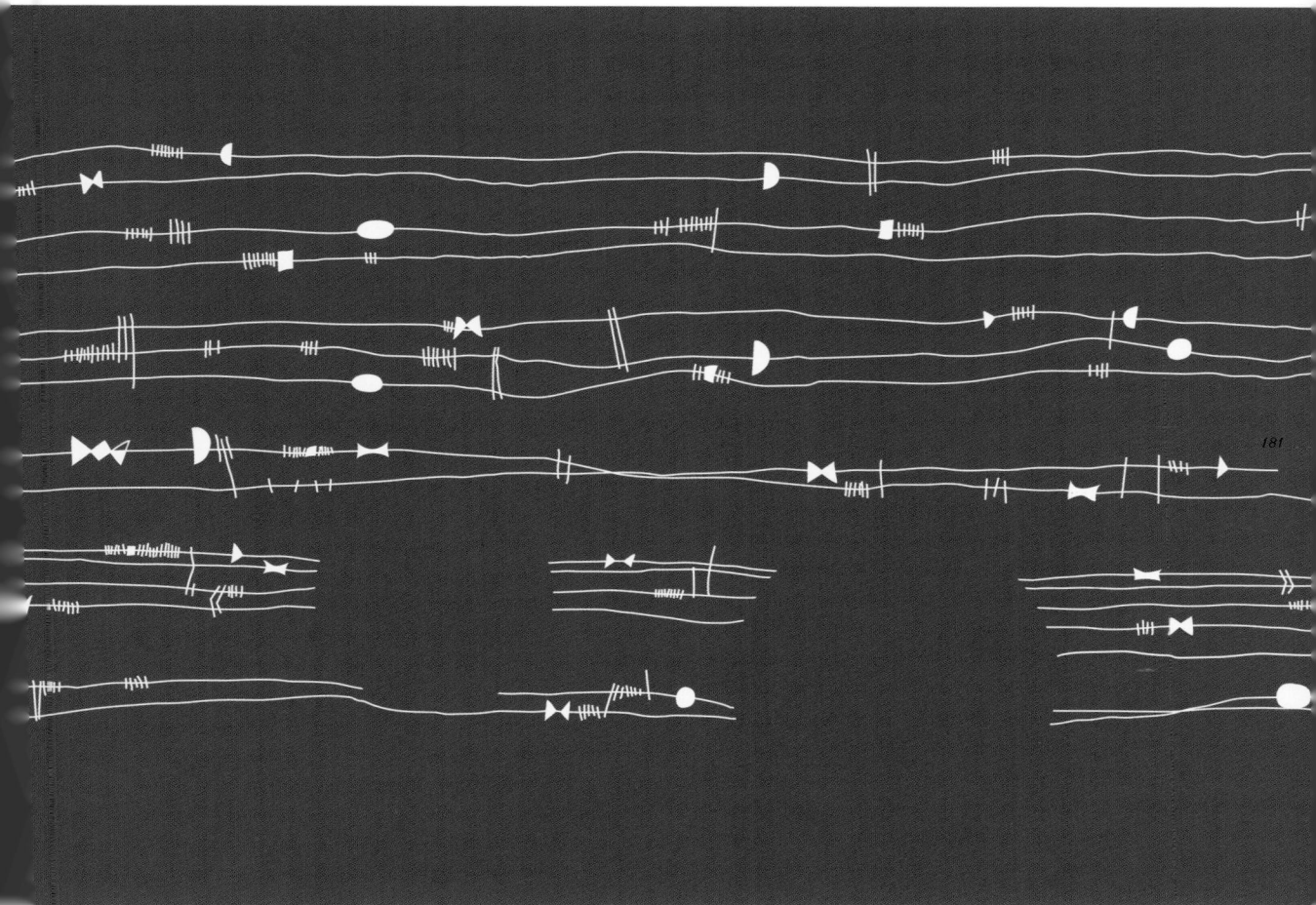

181

182

TITLE: S.Oliver Offices And Showroom
DESIGNER: Studio 63 Architecture + Design
COUNTRY: New York USA
Florence Italy
Hong Kong
Shanghai China

184

TITLE: Energie/Miss Sixty Catania
DESIGNER: Studio 63 Architecture + Design
COUNTRY: Italy

186

TITLE: Updown Court Showflat
DESIGNER: Ching Ping CHANG, Cherry TANG, Louis LAW, Chun Ern YEH, Yu Cheng Wang, Yu You Liao
COUNTRY: Taiwan China

188

TITLE: Yi-Spa-Studio
DESIGNER: Plajer & Franz Studio
COUNTRY: Germany

192

TITLE: Pizza Bar
DESIGNER: Ali Tayar
COUNTRY: USA

194

TITLE: Rios Clementi Hale Studios Office
DESIGNER: Rios Clementi Hale Studios
COUNTRY: USA

TITLE: Building Products Mall - Sea horse
DESIGNER: Design Team - Kalhan Mattoo, Santha Gour Mattoo, Hina Parmar
COUNTRY: India

198

TITLE: YMCA Renaissance Center
DESIGNER: McIntosh Poris Associates
COUNTRY: USA

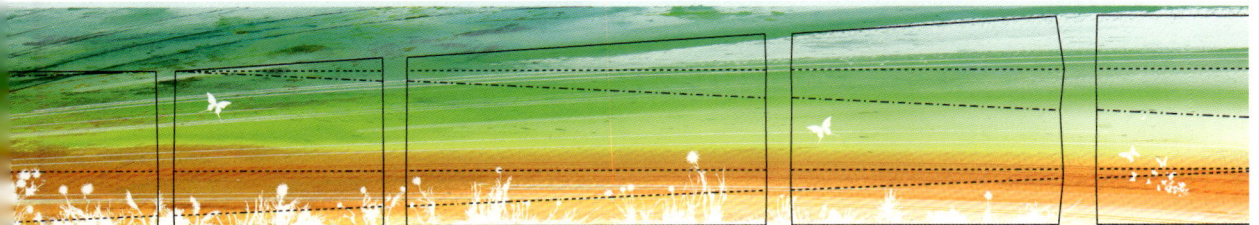

200

201

202

TITLE: Mangrove West Coast
DESIGNER: PTang Studio Ltd
COUNTRY: China

TITLE: Mangrove West Coast
DESIGNER: PTang Studio Ltd
COUNTRY: China

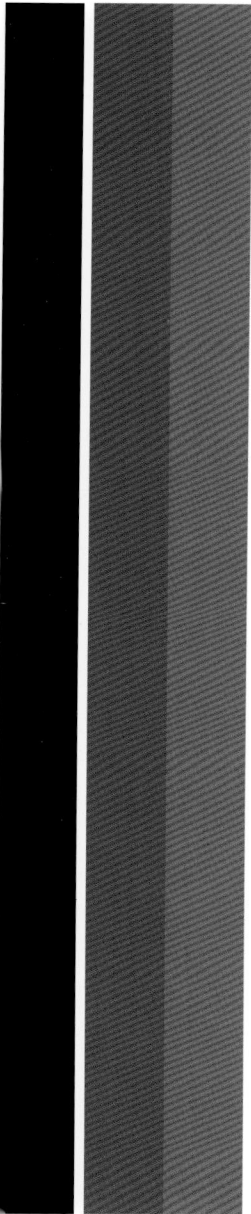

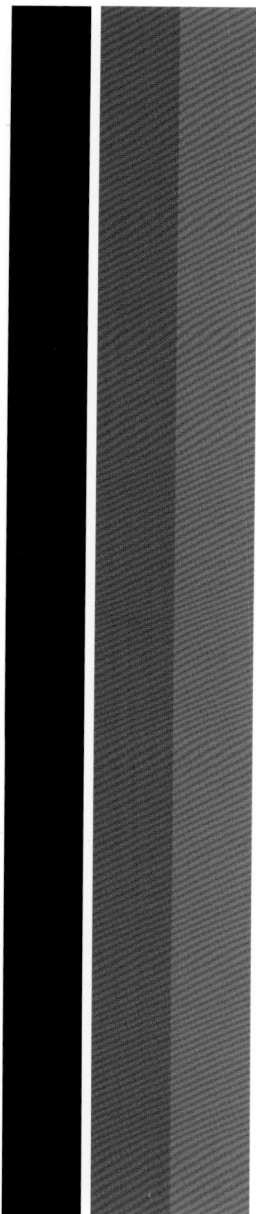

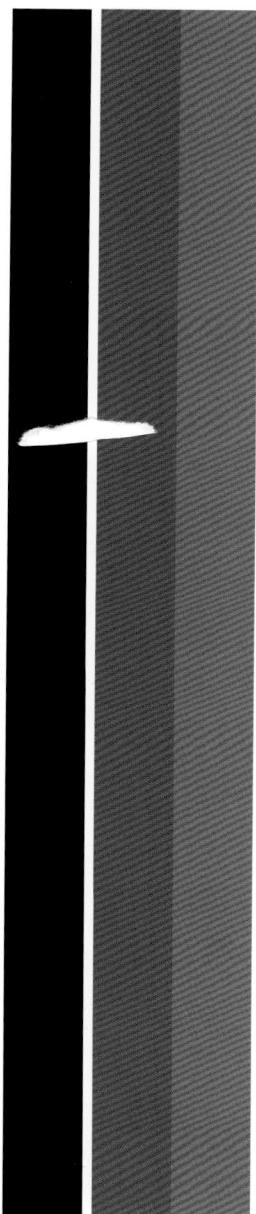

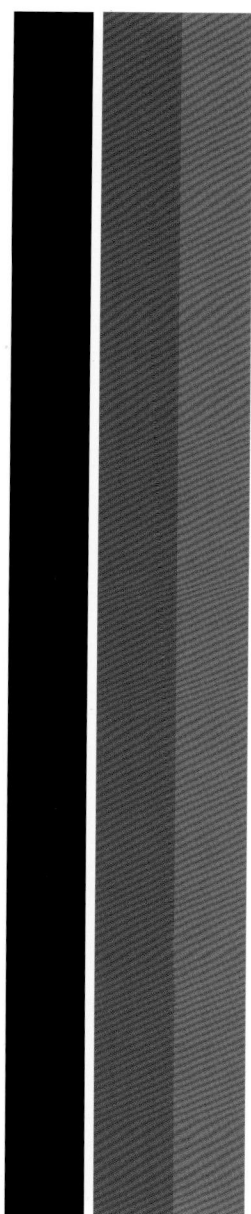

214

TITLE: Office Dupon
DESIGNER: Ramin Visc
COUNTRY: The Netherlands

TITLE: The Fairy Tail Ball Wall
DESIGNER: Funky Little Darlings
COUNTRY: UK

220

TITLE: Born To Sk8
DESIGNER: Funky Little Darlings
COUNTRY: UK

222

224

TITLE: Helter Skelter
DESIGNER: Funky Little Darlings
COUNTRY: UK

TITLE: BMX
DESIGNER: Funky Little Darlings
COUNTRY: UK

226

228

TITLE: Fantasia
DESIGNER: Funky Little Darlings
COUNTRY: UK

TITLE: Ferrari Across Europe
DESIGNER: Funky Little Darlings
COUNTRY: UK

232

TITLE: Fluoro Dragonflies Cowparsley Butterflies And Dandelions
DESIGNER: Funky Little Darlings
COUNTRY: UK

flies, cowparsley, butterflies, dandelions, dragonflies, cowparsley, butterflies, dandelions, dragonfl

236

TITLE: Hotel Fronlas - Room 1 Main Wall Design
DESIGNER: Funky Little Darlings
COUNTRY: UK

TITLE: Hotel Fronlas - Room 2 Main Wall Design
DESIGNER: Funky Little Darlings
COUNTRY: UK

TITLE: Snakes And Ladders

DESIGNER: Funky Little Darlings

COUNTRY: UK

240

242

UK SKATERBOY

uk skaterboy

243

TITLE: Funky Flowers
DESIGNER: Funky Little Darlings
COUNTRY: UK

244

248

249

TITLE: Safari Friends (wall 1)
DESIGNER: Funky Little Darlings
COUNTRY: UK

250

Born to be wild

TITLE: Safari Friends (wall 2)
DESIGNER: Funky Little Darlings
COUNTRY: UK

252

254

TITLE: Tree Of Life
DESIGNER: Funky Little Darlings
COUNTRY: UK

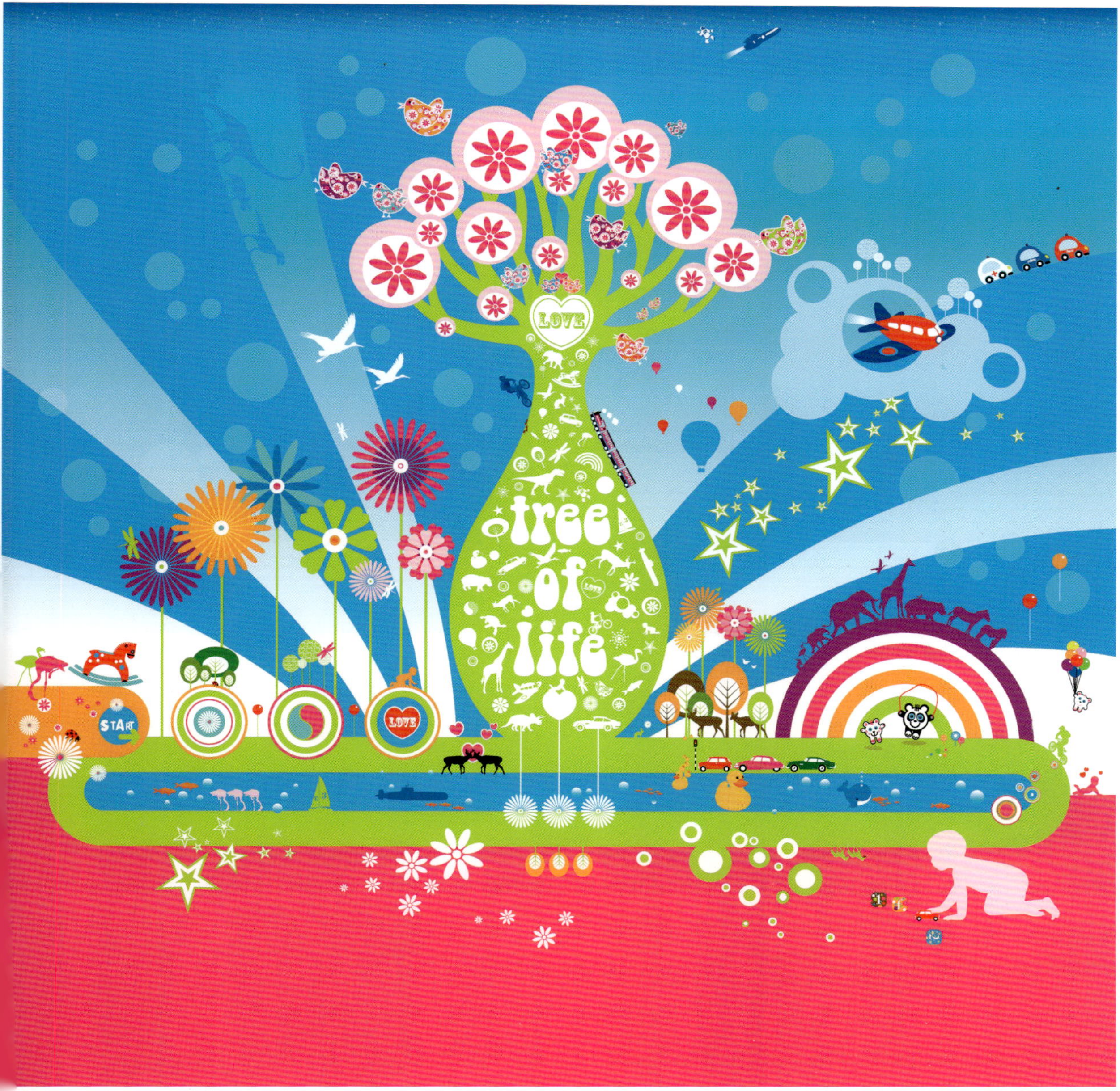
LOVE
tree
of
life
LOVE
START
LOVE

TITLE: Ride The Waves
DESIGNER: Funky Little Darlings
COUNTRY: UK

LIZARD 1

TITLE: Dinosaurs And Aeroplanes
DESIGNER: Funky Little Darlings
COUNTRY: UK

258

TITLE: Fun At The Park
DESIGNER: Funky Little Darlings
COUNTRY: UK

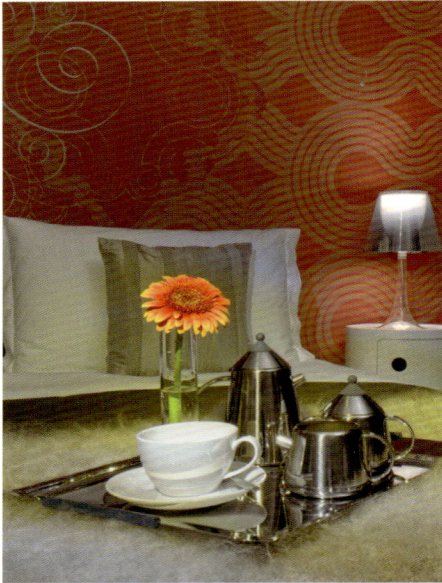

TITLE: Fronlas Hotel Guest Room 1
DESIGNER: Colliss & Quinton
COUNTRY: UK

TITLE: BOSS Orange
DESIGNER: ProjektTriangle Design Studio
COUNTRY: China

TITLE: Witloof
DESIGNER: Maurice Mentjens
COUNTRY: The Netherlands

TITLE: Haymarket Hotel
DESIGNER: Kit Kemp
COUNTRY: UK

TITLE: Outside In
DESIGNER: JOI-Design
COUNTRY: Germany

266

268

TITLE: Le Royal Meridien Restaurant "Le Soleil"
DESIGNER: JOI-Design
COUNTRY: Germany

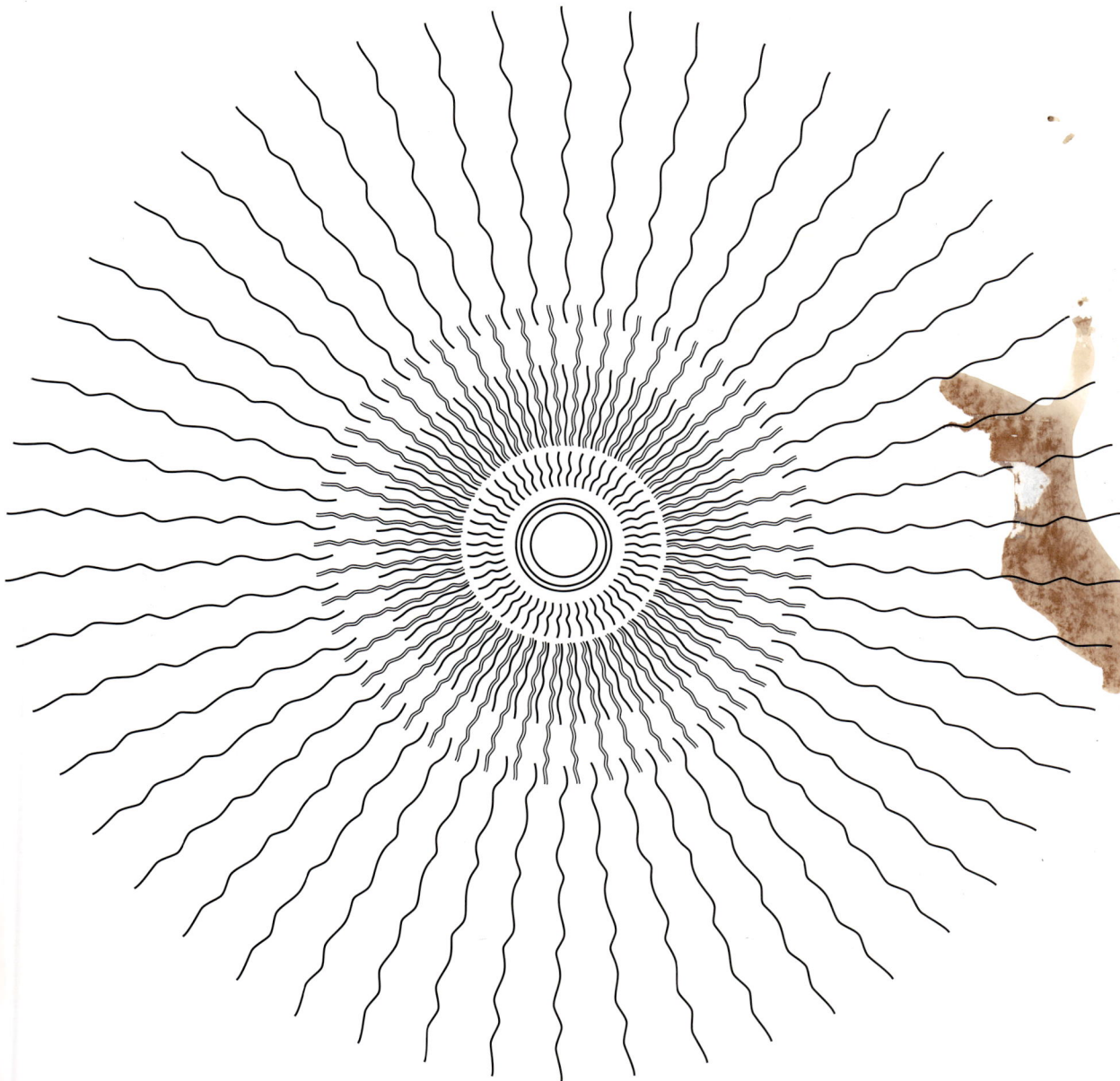

271

TITLE: The Eight
DESIGNER: Steve Leung
COUNTRY: Hongkong China

TITLE: The Eight
DESIGNER: Steve Leung
COUNTRY: Hongkong China

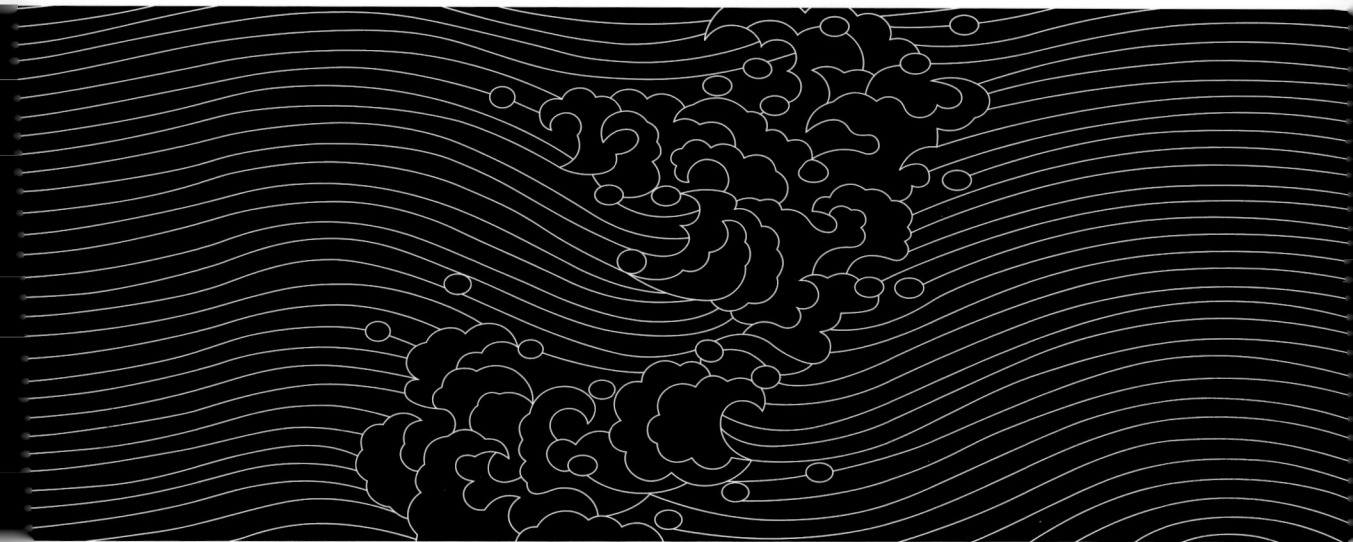

276

TITLE: The Eight
DESIGNER: Steve Leung
COUNTRY: Hongkong China

278

TITLE: The Eight
DESIGNER: Steve Leung
COUNTRY: Hongkong China

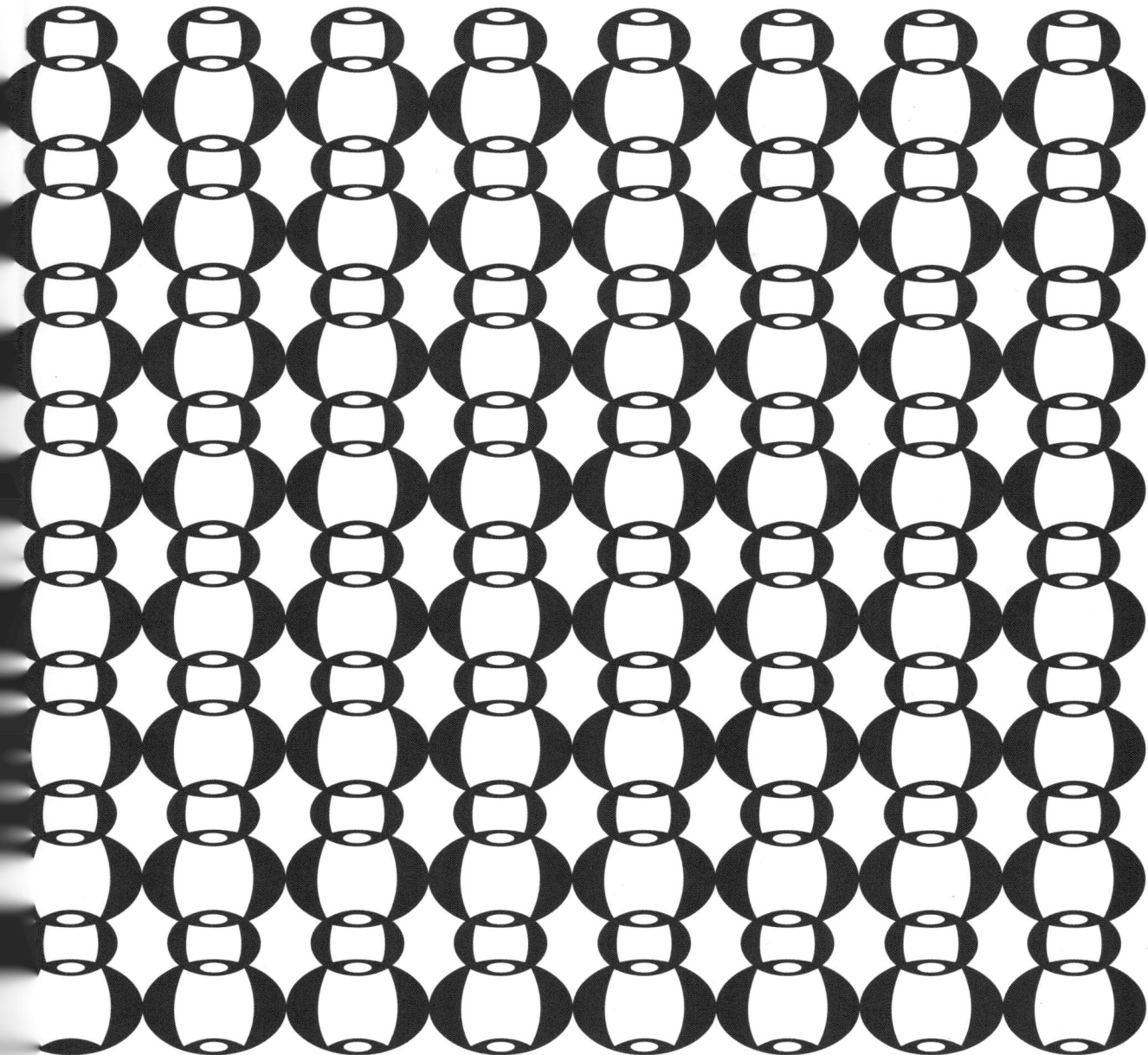

TITLE: Hotel Watt 13
DESIGNER: Caberlon Caroppi Hotel Design
COUNTRY: Italy

282

TITLE: Branches And Leaves
DESIGNER: Futao Liu
COUNTRY: China

284

285

TITLE: Flower
DESIGNER: Futao Liu
COUNTRY: China

TITLE: Calligraphica Collection
DESIGNER: Macrina Busato Studio
COUNTRY: Spain

288

CASIO

294

TITLE: Casio Store
DESIGNER: Brinkworth/Germ/CheethamBEll JWT
COUNTRY: UK

TITLE: Casio Store
DESIGNER: Brinkworth/Germ/CheethamBEll JWT
COUNTRY: UK

296

CASIO

297

TITLE: The Deutsche Bank Lounge
DESIGNER: Karim Rashid
COUNTRY: Germany
PHOTOGRAPHER: Lukas Roth

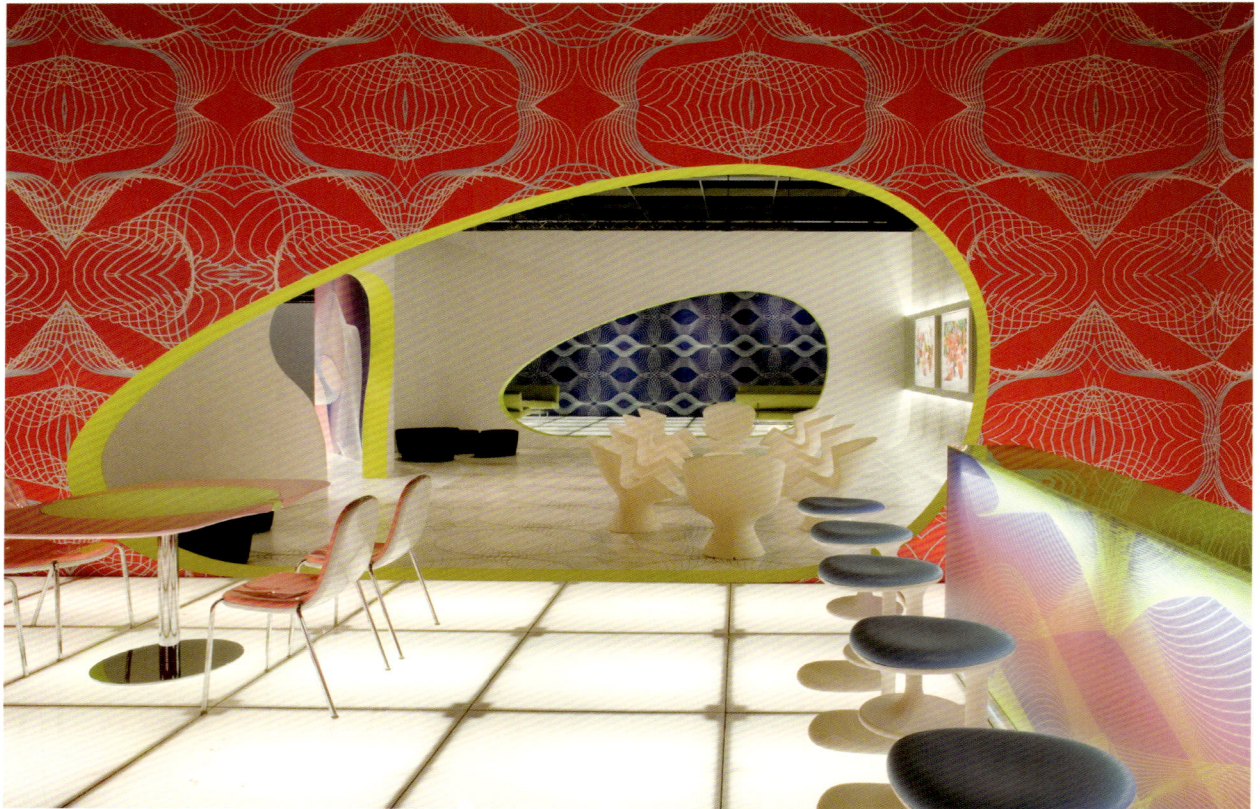

300

TITLE: The Deutsche Bank Lounge
DESIGNER: Karim Rashid
COUNTRY: Germany
PHOTOGRAPHER: Lukas Roth

TITLE: Cubion Office
DESIGNER: Jackie-B
COUNTRY: Denmark

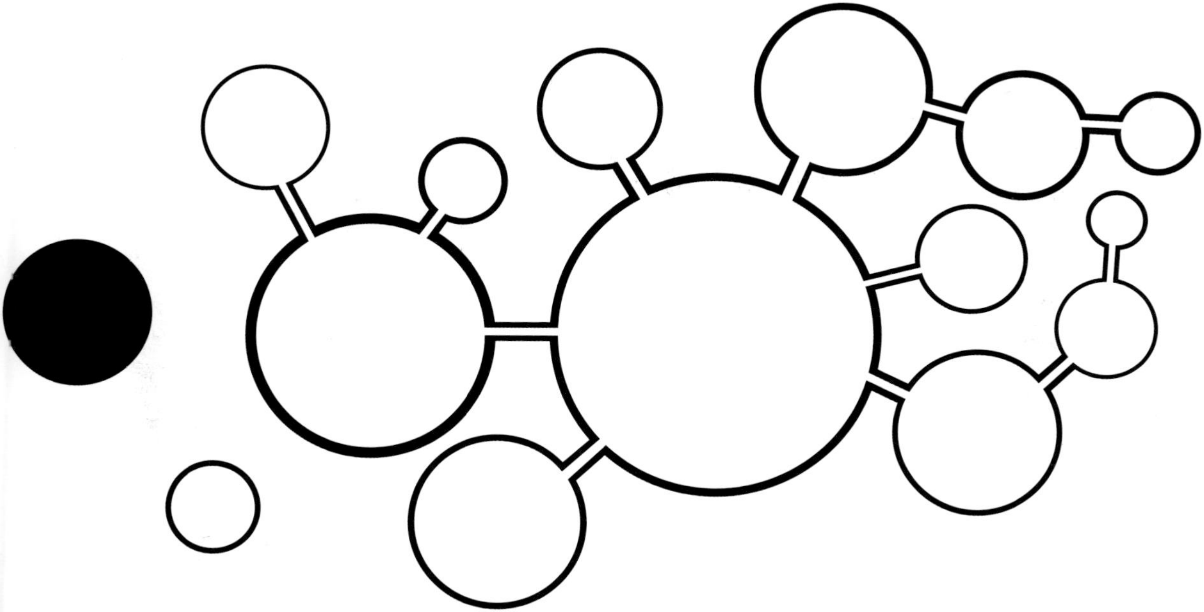